Geology Rocks!

Soil

Rebecca Faulkner

www.raintreepublishers.co.uk

Visit our website to find out more information about **Raintree** books.

To order:
☎ Phone 44 (0) 1865 888112
🖹 Send a fax to 44 (0) 1865 314091
🖥 Visit the Raintree bookshop at **www.raintreepublishers.co.uk** to browse our catalogue and order online.

First published in Great Britain by Raintree,
Halley Court, Jordan Hill, Oxford OX2 8EJ,
part of Harcourt Education.
Raintree is a registered trademark
of Harcourt Education Ltd.

Editorial: Kathryn Walker, Melanie Waldron, and
Rachel Howells
Design: Victoria Bevan, Rob Norridge,
and AMR Design Ltd (www.amrdesign.com)
Illustrations: David Woodroffe
Picture Research: Melissa Allison and Mica Brancic
Production: Duncan Gilbert
Originated by Chroma Graphics Pte. Ltd
Printed and bound in China by
South China Printing Company

ISBN 978 1406 20903 7 (hardback)
12 11 10 09 08
10 9 8 7 6 5 4 3 2 1

ISBN 978 1406 20911 2 (paperback)
13 12 11 10 09
10 9 8 7 6 5 4 3 2 1

**British Library Cataloguing in
Publication Data**
Faulkner, Rebecca.
  Soil. – (Geology Rocks!)
  552.5
A full catalogue record for this book is available
from the British Library.

This levelled text is a version of *Freestyle: Geology Rocks: Soil.*

Acknowledgements
The publishers would like to thank the following for
permission to reproduce photographs:

©Arctic Photo p. **33**; ©Ardea p. **32** (Bob Gibbons);
©Corbis pp. **5, 6, 30, 37, 41 top, 44**, p. **16** (David
Aubrey), p. **13** (Guenter Rossenbach), p. **9** (Joel W.
Rogers), p. **26** (Robert Llewellyn), p.**39** (Sally A.
Morgan), p. **38** (Yann Arthus-Bertrand); ©FLPA p. **28
left** (Gary K. Smith), p. **31** (Holt/Primrose Peacock),
p. **15** (Nigel Cattlin); ©Geo Science Features Picture
Library pp. **5 top inset, 5 middle inset, 7, 8,
17, 18, 20 left, 20 right, 22, 27, 34, 35** (Prof. B.
Booth); ©Getty Images p. **40** (John and Lisa Merrill),
pp. **5 bottom, 42** (Robert Harding World Imagery/
Jochen Schlenker), p. **28 right** (Stone); ©Masterfile
p. **36** (Dale Wilson), p. **21** (Ledingham/Boden);
©NHPA p. **4** (Stephen Dalton); ©Photolibrary.com
p. **43** (Jon Arnold); ©Science Photo Library p. **12**
(Bruce M. Herman), p. **14** (David Scharf), p. **25**
(Joyce Photographics), p. **41 bottom** (Michael
Marten), p. **10** (Simon Fraser)

Cover photograph of a seedbed ridged for flood
irrigation, California, USA reproduced with
permission of ©FLPA (Nigel Cattlin).

Every effort has been made to contact copyright
holders of any material reproduced in this book.
Any omissions will be rectified in subsequent
printings if notice is given to the publishers.

Disclaimer
All the Internet addresses (URLs) given in this book
were valid at the time of going to press. However,
due to the dynamic nature of the Internet, some
addresses may have changed, or sites may have
changed or ceased to exist since publication. While
the author and publishers regret any inconvenience
this may cause readers, no responsibility for any
such changes can be accepted by either the author
or the publishers.

Contents

Any words appearing in the text in bold, **like this,** are explained in the glossary. You can also look out for them in the **On the rocks!** section at the bottom of each page.

THE WONDERS OF SOIL

Earthworms
There can be more than a million earthworms in half a hectare (1 acre) of land. This is an area about the size of a football pitch.

You probably know that soil is a crumbly material. Plants can grow in it. But did you know that millions of creatures live in soil? Did you know that soil forms from rocks?

Soil forms very slowly. It can take thousands of years for rock to change into soil. But soil that has formed can be washed away by rain. It can be blown away by wind. This movement of soil is called **soil erosion.**

⬇ **Earthworms eat soil as they burrow through it.**

soil erosion   movement of soil away from where it formed. The soil is blown or washed away.

Soil is very important to us. We need it to grow our food. Humans have grown crops in soil for thousands of years.

But in some places crop growing has increased soil erosion. This is because the soil is less protected from wind and rain. **Eroded** soil produces fewer crops. It is causing big problems for farmers.

Find out later...

...how volcanoes are good for soil.

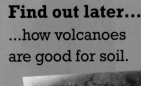

...what types of animals live in soil.

...how these trees protect soil.

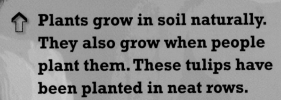
⬆ Plants grow in soil naturally. They also grow when people plant them. These tulips have been planted in neat rows.

ROCKY SOIL

Soil covers much of Earth's surface. You can see soil in forests and parks. In other places it is covered by grass or roads. Below the soil are rocks.

Different soils

You may think that all soil is brown. But it also comes in black or grey. It can be red or yellow. It can even be white.

What is soil?

Soil starts to form when rocks are broken down. They break down into tiny pieces. These rock pieces mix with plants and tiny animals. They also mix with water and air. Then soil is formed.

Nutrients in soil

Minerals are substances that are found in nature. Rocks are made up of lots of minerals. As rocks break down, minerals enter the soil.

⇩ This soil is thin and rocky. Very little will grow in it.

mineral substance found in nature. Rocks are made from lots of minerals.

Minerals provide **nutrients**. These are substances that plants and animals in the soil need. They need nutrients to live and grow.

These plants and animals die and rot away. Then the nutrients they contain return to the soil.

Useful ash
Sometimes ash comes out of volcanoes (see photo below). This ash contains lots of nutrients. It settles and forms soil. It forms some of the best soil for growing plants.

How does rock become soil?

Rocks at Earth's surface are attacked by rain and wind. They are also attacked by ice. Pieces of rock are broken off. This is called **weathering**. It happens over thousands of years.

There are two main ways in which rocks break down to form soil:

- physical weathering
- chemical weathering.

⇩ These broken rocks are known as **scree**. They have been broken by frost shattering. Over time scree will turn into soil.

Physical weathering

Frost shattering is a type of physical weathering. It happens when rainwater gets into cracks in rocks. When the water freezes it expands (gets bigger). Then the rock is forced apart. It shatters.

Chemical weathering

Rocks are made up of materials called **minerals**. Rain can dissolve some of these minerals. They dissolve like sugar in a glass of water. The rock will then crumble. This is called chemical weathering.

Tree roots

Sometimes plant roots grow into cracks in rocks (see photo below). These roots can break the rock apart. This is another type of physical weathering.

scree   broken rock fragments. Scree is usually found on mountain slopes.

Mixing the rock

The pieces of broken rock do not always stay in one place. Some of the pieces may be picked up by wind or water. They may be picked up by glaciers (rivers of ice). Then the bits of rock are dumped in a new place.

All these pieces of rock form a loose layer on Earth's surface. This is called **regolith**. Tiny plants and animals may live in the regolith. When they die their remains rot. They form **organic matter**.

At some time this river has flooded. It dropped the broken rock it was carrying. This rock is at the side of the river. Over time it will become soil.

Organic matter mixes with the regolith to form soil. When there is enough organic matter, plants can grow. Animals that feed on the plants then move in.

These plants and animals also die and rot. Their remains add more organic matter to the soil.

Water in the soil continues to break down the rock below. This rock is called the **parent rock**. It is the rock that the soil forms from. It breaks down to produce more soil.

⬇ **These pictures show how rocks break down to form soil. This process takes thousands of years.**

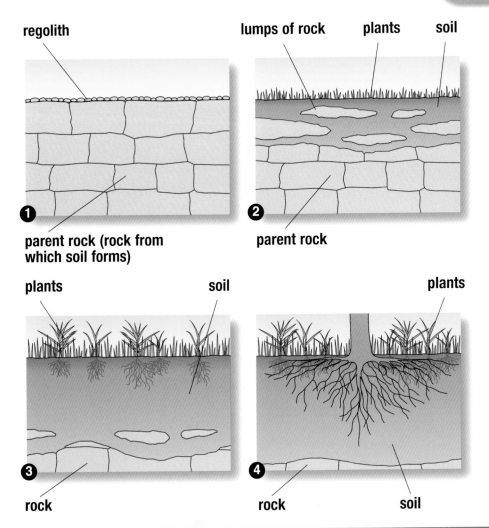

regolith

parent rock (rock from which soil forms)

lumps of rock   **plants**   **soil**

parent rock

plants   **soil**

rock

plants

rock   **soil**

WHAT CAN WE FIND IN SOIL?

Soil is a mixture of many things. These include:

- rock particles (pieces of rock)
- air
- water
- **organic matter** (remains of plants and animals).

Rock particles

Rock breaks down to form soil. This rock is known as the **parent rock**. Broken pieces of parent rock form the main part of soil.

These rock particles can be different sizes. Some may be as big as pebbles. Other particles may be smaller than sand.

⬇ **These are granite rocks. It will take thousands of years to break them down into soil.**

Air and water

The spaces between clumps of soil are called **pores**. Pores contain air or water. Animals and plants in the soil need this air and water. They need it to live and grow.

Sometimes soil is very wet. Then most of the pores are filled with water. This leaves little room for air. We say this soil is **waterlogged**.

⇩ This soil contains too much water. Puddles have formed. When this happens we say that the soil is waterlogged.

Organic matter

Soil can be full of life. Animals and plants live in soil. So do **bacteria** and **fungi**. Bacteria and fungi are very tiny living things.

When the plants and animals die they rot away. They form **organic matter**. Organic matter puts **nutrients** back into the soil. Nutrients are substances that living things need to grow.

Bacteria

Soil contains billions of tiny bacteria. The bacteria are known as **decomposers**. This is because they help

⇩ These are tiny bacteria that live in soil. This is what they look like under a **microscope**. A microscope makes things look bigger.

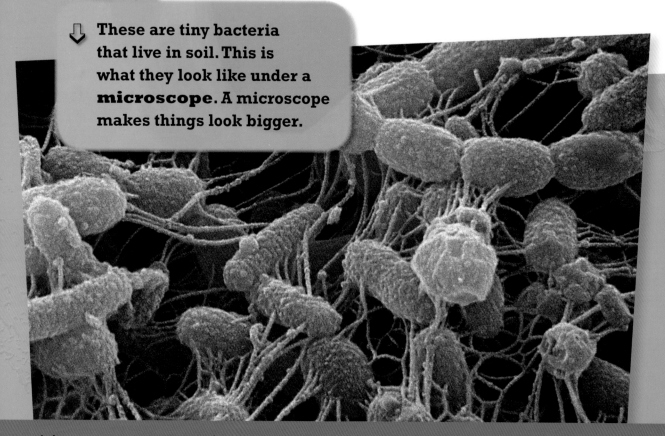

decompose (break down) things. They help break down the dead animals and plants.

Fungi

Some types of fungi are also decomposers. They help bacteria to break down dead plants and animals.

Other types of of fungi grow on plant roots. These fungi have thin hairs called **hyphae**. Hyphae spread through the soil. They search out water and nutrients. This helps the plant get food and water.

⬇ **Many different types of fungi grow in soil. These mushrooms are a type of fungi.**

hyphae thin hairs on fungi

Plants

Plant roots collect water and **nutrients** from soil. Nutrients are substances that plants need to grow. Plant roots grip the soil. They hold the soil together. This helps stop **soil erosion**. Soil erosion is when soil particles are washed or blown away.

When the plant dies it rots away. This returns nutrients to the soil.

Animals

Lots of animals live in soil. They include earthworms and termites. They also include badgers and moles. All these animals move through soil.

⬅ **This plant is getting the water and nutrients it needs. It gets them through its roots.**

As the animals move they mix up the soil. They also make spaces for air and water.

Earthworms eat soil as they move along. They leave chewed up soil behind as droppings. This helps to break down **organic matter** (dead plants and animals) in the soil.

⇩ This huge pile of soil is a termite mound. Millions of termites live in the soil under it.

soil erosion   movement of soil away from where it formed. The soil is blown or washed away.

17

Humus

Dead leaves pile up on the ground. **Bacteria** and **fungi** (see pages 14 and 15) break down these leaves. They also break down dead grasses and animals. This forms a dark, sticky substance. It is called **humus**.

Humus is a source of **nutrients**. These are substances that plants and animals in the soil need. Humus also acts like glue. It holds the soil together. This helps prevent the soil being washed or blown away.

⬇ **Over time these leaves will turn into humus. This is how trees return nutrients to the soil.**

humus   mashed up, rotting remains of dead plants and animals in soil

Humus forms near the top of soil. This is why the soil you see is usually dark.

Animals, such as earthworms, burrow into the soil. As they burrow they take the humus with them. This mixes nutrients into the deeper soil. Plant roots can get at the nutrients there.

Peat
Peat is a type of soil that contains a lot of humus. People sometimes add it to the soil in their yards. Peat helps their plants to grow.

⬇ **This diagram shows what an average soil sample contains.**

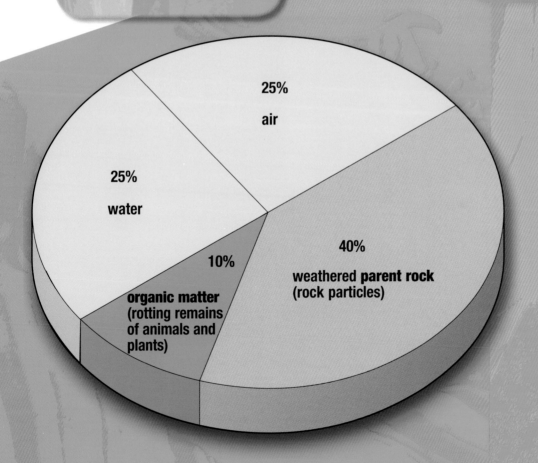

25%
air

25%
water

10%
organic matter
(rotting remains of animals and plants)

40%
weathered **parent rock**
(rock particles)

WHAT DOES SOIL FEEL LIKE?

Soil may feel rough or smooth. How it feels depends on the size of the particles (tiny pieces) in the soil. These particles can be sand, silt, or clay.

Sandy soil

A soil that contains lots of sand feels gritty. Its particles do not stick together well.

Sand particles are one of the larger types of particles. There are large **pores** (spaces) between them. Water drains quickly through sandy soil.

The picture on the left shows sand grains. There are large spaces between the grains in sandy soil. The picture below shows clay soil. The grains in clay are tightly packed together.

particles are tightly packed

clay soil

Silty soil

Silt particles are finer than sand. Silty soil feels smooth like soap. It holds together better than sandy soil. This is because the pores are smaller. Water takes longer to drain through.

Clay soil

Clay soil feels wet and sticky. Clay particles are tiny. You need a **microscope** to see them. Clay particles trap lots of water. Clay soil is often **waterlogged** or full of water.

This is sandy soil. It is loose and light.

waterlogged   filled with water. A waterlogged soil has pores full of water.

21

WHAT DOES SOIL LOOK LIKE?

Air and water

The amount of water or air a soil holds is important for growing plants. This depends on the size of soil particles. It also depends on the soil structure.

Soil sticks together in lumps. These are called **peds**. Soil structure is the way that soil holds together. This depends on the type of ped. There are four types:

- crumb
- platy
- blocky
- columnar

Crumb

A crumb structure is best for plant growth. The peds are about the size of breadcrumbs. There are lots of air and water spaces.

Platy

A platy structure is bad for plant growth. The peds are flat and stacked together. There are few air spaces. Plant roots cannot get through.

⇨ **This soil has a crumb structure. It is good for growing plants.**

Blocky

In some soils the peds are a mixture of shapes and sizes. This is called a blocky structure.

Columnar

Columnar soils have peds shaped like columns. There are some air and water spaces. This type of structure is usually found in deep soil.

Different structures
Soils can have one or more structures. The structure may change at different depths.

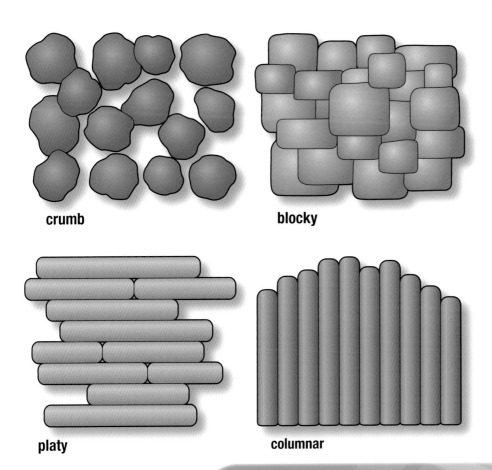

crumb

blocky

platy

columnar

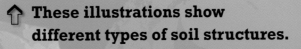

⬆ These illustrations show different types of soil structures.

Soil layers

Soil is made up of different layers. These layers are called **horizons**. If you could slice through the ground you would see them. Together the different soil horizons form what is called a **soil profile**.

A horizon

The **A horizon** is the top layer. It is sometimes called topsoil. This is where plants grow and animals live. **Humus** forms here (see page 18).

Rainwater enters the soil in the A horizon. The water picks up **nutrients** from the humus. Nutrients are substances that plants and animals need to live.

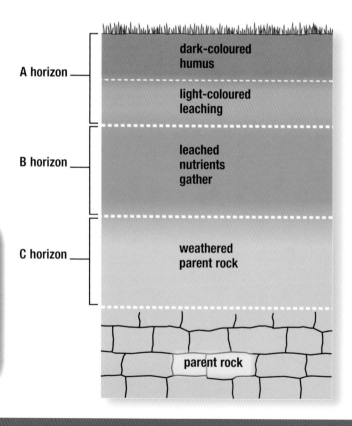

A horizon — dark-coloured humus

light-coloured leaching

B horizon — leached nutrients gather

C horizon — weathered parent rock

parent rock

⇨ **This is an example of a soil profile. The depth and colour of the layers can differ in different soils.**

The water drains through this layer to **B horizon**. It carries the nutrients with it. This is called **leaching**.

B horizon

The B horizon is where nutrients gather. Plant roots reach down into the B horizon for food and water.

C horizon

The **C horizon** can be very deep. It is completely made up of rock particles. It is too deep for plants and animals to live in.

Parent rock

Parent rock lies underneath the soil. This is solid rock. It is the rock that soil forms from.

Coloured layers
The A horizon tends to be darker than the other layers. This is because it contains more humus. The B horizon will be different colours in different soils.

⇦ **You can tell the different layers of soil by their different colours.**

How can we study soil?

Scientists who study soil are called **pedologists**. Maybe you can dig up a sample of soil. Then you can be a pedologist too.

- See if you can identify any **horizons** in the soil (see page 24–25).

- Rub some soil between your fingers. What **texture** (feel) does it have?

- Look at the shape of the **peds** (clumps of soil). Which of the types of peds on pages 22 and 23 are they like?

- Can you see any plants or animals in your soil?

⇩ You can feel the texture of the soil by rubbing it with your fingers.

Why do pedologists study soil?

Soil takes thousands of years to form. Farmers know they must treat it carefully. Otherwise they may have problems growing crops.

Pedologists can find out what the soil is like in an area. Then they can tell the farmers what crops can be grown there. Pedologists can also tell farmers how to improve their soil.

⇩ This is a **soil auger**. It is a tool made like a screw. A soil auger is used to collect soil samples from different layers.

Soil all over Earth

There are thousands of different types of soil across the world. Scientists put these soils into different groups. One way of grouping soil is by **climate**. Climate is the weather pattern in an area.

Climate and soil

Climate affects the type of soil that forms. In a wet climate the soil **pores** (spaces) may be filled with water. In a dry climate the soil contains little water.

The type of plants that grow in an area depends on the climate. The type of plants affects how much **humus** can form (see page 18).

⇨ **Different climates produce different types of soil.**

The climate also affects how quickly **parent rock** breaks down. Parent rock is the rock that soil forms from. **Weathering** (breaking down) usually happens more quickly in hot, wet climates.

Climates and soils

There are many different climates in the world. Each has its own type of soil.

Climate	Soil type
temperate	black earth, brown earth
polar	podsol, tundra
tropical	ferralsol, laterite, desert
mediterranean	brown earth/desert

This map shows where the different soils are found.

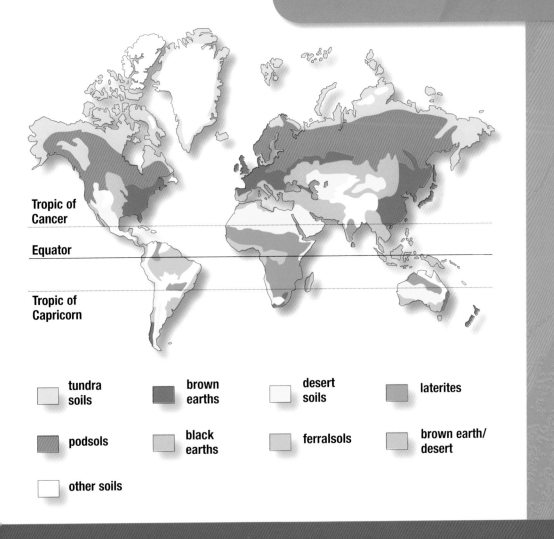

Tropic of Cancer

Equator

Tropic of Capricorn

- tundra soils
- brown earths
- desert soils
- laterites
- podsols
- black earths
- ferralsols
- brown earth/ desert
- other soils

Temperate regions

Temperate regions are areas where the temperatures are neither extremely hot or extremely cold. These regions have two types of soil:

• black earths   • brown earths.

Black earths

Black earths are found in temperate grasslands. Grasslands are areas where the main plants growing are grasses. Black earths contain more **humus** (see page 18) than any other soil. Black earth is the best soil for farming.

⬇ Black earths are found here in the prairies of North America. They are the best soils in the world for farming.

Brown earths

Brown earths form under forests in temperate regions. Dead leaves form lots of humus. The **A horizon** (top layer) is usually dark brown.

There are plenty of spaces in brown earths. When rainfall is heavy, brown earths may suffer from too much **leaching**. This is when water drains through the soil taking the **nutrients** with it. Nutrients are substances that plants need to grow.

⇩ **This tree is growing well in brown earth. Its roots can go deep into the soil.**

Polar regions

Polar regions are the coldest parts of the world. These regions have two types of soil:

- podsols
- tundra soil.

Podsols

Podsols are found in northern parts of the countries of Russia and Canada. They are found under **coniferous** forests. The leaves on coniferous trees usually stay green throughout the year.

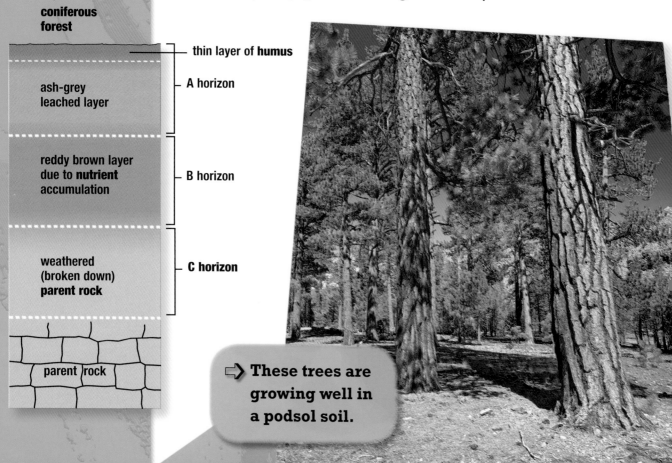

coniferous forest

thin layer of **humus**

A horizon

ash-grey leached layer

reddy brown layer due to **nutrient** accumulation

B horizon

weathered (broken down) **parent rock**

C horizon

parent rock

⇨ **These trees are growing well in a podsol soil.**

coniferous to do with conifers. Conifers are trees that usually stay green all the year round.

These areas have high rainfall. This causes lots of **leaching** (see page 31). The **A horizon** (top layer) is often pale coloured. The **B horizon** (layer below) is often reddish brown.

Tundra soils

In areas further north the **climates** are colder. The soil may be frozen for most of the year.

In summer the surface melts. But the soil below stays frozen. Water cannot flow through. Because of this the surface becomes **waterlogged**. This soil is called tundra soil.

⇩ **This tundra soil has become waterlogged.**

humus mashed up, rotting remains of dead plants and animals in soil

Tropical regions

Tropical regions are the hottest parts of the world. These regions have three types of soil:

• ferralsols   • laterites   • desert soils.

Ferralsols

Some tropical areas have hot, wet **climates**. Soils can be up to 30 metres (100 feet) deep. These are called ferralsols.

Iron soil

Ferral means "iron". Ferralsols get their name because they contain a lot of the **mineral** iron. The iron makes them a red colour (see picture below).

Heavy rain causes a lot of **leaching**. This is when water drains through soil quickly. It takes the **nutrients** with it. Plants need these nutrients to grow.

Laterites

Laterite soils are found in the grasslands of tropical regions. These areas have wet and dry seasons. In the wet season leaching is very strong. It causes a hard layer of soil to form below the surface. This is called laterite.

Desert soils

Some tropical areas have hot, dry climates. The soils there are thin and often very dry. This means the soil is easily **eroded** (blown away).

Brick-like soil
Laterite is so hard that it can be cut into blocks. These can be used for building houses.

⇩ **This is desert soil. Little can grow in this soil.**

mineral substance found in nature. Rocks are made from lots of minerals.

USING SOIL

We use soil mainly for farming. Farmers produce crops that provide food. Without soil there would be nothing to eat.

The perfect soil for farming?

Sandy soil is good for growing crops. It has large **pores** (spaces). Water and air flow through them. But sandy soil lacks **nutrients**. These are the substances that plants need to grow. Water carries nutrients away as it drains through.

Long roots
Plants with long roots are suited to sandy soil. Their roots stretch down into the deeper soil. This is where the water and nutrients are.

⇨ **This area has good loamy soil. It produces good crops.**

Silty soil (see page 21) is also good for growing crops. It has smaller pores than sandy soil. These trap water and nutrients. But silty soil **erodes** easily. The top layer is easily blown or washed away.

The perfect soil for crop growing is a mix of sand, silt, and clay. Its spaces are big enough for air and water to enter. But clay makes the soil stick into clumps. These hold on to nutrients. This soil is called **loam**.

Fertilizers
Over time crops will use up all nutrients in the soil. This is why farmers add **fertilizers** to soil. Fertilizers put nutrients back into soil.

⬇ **This aeroplane is spraying crops with liquid fertilizer.**

How are we destroying soil?

Soil erosion is when soil is washed or blown away. It takes thousands of years to happen. It also takes thousands of years for soil to form. So there should be a balance between soil formation and erosion.

But human activities are making soil erosion happen quicker. Soil is now **eroding** (moving away) faster than it can form.

Cutting down trees

The main cause of soil erosion is **deforestation**. This is when trees are cut down. They are cut down to make way for farming or houses.

⇨ **This is the country of Madagascar. Deforestation has caused soil to be washed into the rivers. The soil has turned them red.**

Without trees the soil has no protection from wind and rain. There are no roots to hold the soil together. The soil quickly becomes infertile. This means that crops cannot grow in it.

In this way huge areas of forest are being turned into wasteland. Nothing can grow there.

⬇ This is an area of tropical forest that has been cleared. The soil here is easily eroded.

Bad farming

Sometimes farmers keep too many animals in the same field. They eat too much grass. This is called **overgrazing**. The bare soil has no protection from wind and rain. It is easily washed or blown away.

Many farmers grow the same crop each year. This uses up **nutrients** in the soil. Plants need nutrients to grow. Farmers then need to add **fertilizers** to the soil. Fertlizers put back the nutrients.

⇩ **Overgrazing is turning this land into desert.**

overgrazing keeping too many animals in one area of land, so they eat too much of the grass

But it is easy to use too much fertilizer. Then rain will wash it into lakes or rivers.

Fertilizer causes too much **algae** to grow in the water. Algae are tiny green plants. They use up all the oxygen in the water. Oxygen is a gas that fish need to live. With no oxygen left for them, the fish die.

Farm machinery

Farmers often use large, heavy farm machinery. This squashes down the soil. Then there are not enough spaces in the soil for plants to grow.

⇐ **Heavy farm machinery like this squashes the soil.**

⇨ **This pond is full of algae. This is because fertilizer has got into the pond.**

How can we protect soil?

Soil erosion happens when soil is washed or blown away. Nothing will grow in **eroded** soil.

Farmers have ways of reducing soil erosion. They plant trees to replace the ones they cut down. Trees hold the soil together. Their leaves protect the soil from rain.

When farmers gather in the crops they can leave behind parts that are not needed. These can help soil in two ways:

- they protect the soil from the wind and rain
- they rot and return **nutrients** to the soil.

Farmers can also grow different crops each year. These crops use up different nutrients. This way the same nutrients are not removed from the soil each year.

Farmers can also plant "cover crops" in some fields. These are crops that cover the soil, such as clover. They are allowed to rot away. This puts nutrients back into the soil.

Terraces

On steep slopes, rain can easily wash the soil downhill. Making **terraces** can help stop this. Terraces are like steps cut into the slope.

⬇ **Crops grow along these terraces. The water soaks into the soil instead of running downhill.**

terrace step cut into steep land. It can be used for growing crops.

SUMMARY

- Earth's land surface is covered in soil. It is home to many plants and animals.

- Soil forms as rock is weathered (broken down). The rock pieces mix with dead plants and animals. They also mix with water and air.

- **Parent rock** is the rock that soil forms from. Soil builds up above the parent rock. It forms layers called **horizons**.

- There are many types of soil in the world. Soil is made up of particles (small pieces) of different sizes. These clump together to form **peds**.

- **Soil erosion** is when soil is blown or washed away. In some places the soil is being **eroded** faster than it can form.

- We need need soil to grow our food. It is important that we protect the world's soil.

← These crops are growing in **loam**. This is the best type of soil for farming.

FIND OUT MORE

Books

The Amazing World of Microlife: Microlife That Lives in Soil, Steve Parker (Raintree Publishers, 2006)

Earth's Precious Resources: Soil, Ian Graham (Heinemann Library, 2005)

Hidden Life: What's Living in Your Backyard?, Andrew Solway (Heinemann Library, 2004)

Sand and Soil, Beth Gurney (Crabtree Publishing Company, 2004)

Using the Internet

If you want to find out more about minerals you can search the Internet. Try using keywords such as these:

- earthworm
- soil erosion
- soil profile.

You can also use different keywords. Try choosing some words from this book.

Try using a search directory such as www.yahooligans.com

Search tips

There are billions of pages on the Internet. It can be difficult to find what you are looking for. These search skills will help you find useful websites more quickly:

- Know exactly what you want to find out about.
- Use two to six keywords in a search. Put the most important words first.
- Only use names of people, places, or things.

GLOSSARY

A horizon top layer of soil

algae tiny plants

B horizon layer of soil below the top layer. This is where nutrients gather.

bacteria tiny organisms that live in soil and break down dead plants and animals

C horizon deep layer of soil. It is completely made up of broken pieces of rock.

climate pattern of weather in an area

coniferous to do with conifers. Conifers are trees that usually stay green all the year round.

decompose break down dead plants and animals

decomposer organism that breaks down dead plants and animals

deforestation cutting down trees and removing them

erode remove by wind or rain

fertilizer substance that is added to soil to improve its fertility

fungi tiny organisms that live in soil

horizon layer in soil

humus mashed up, rotting remains of dead plants and animals in soil

hyphae thin hairs on fungi

leaching process where water drains through soil, taking minerals with it

loam perfect soil for crop growth

microscope device used to see very small objects. It makes them appear bigger.

mineral substance found in nature. Rocks are made from lots of minerals.

nutrient important mineral needed by a plant for growth

organic matter rotting remains of plants and animals

overgrazing keeping too many animals in one area of land, so they eat too much of the grass

parent rock rock from which soil forms

ped clump of soil

pedologist scientist who studies soil

pore space between clumps of soil

regolith loose layer of weathered rock on the surface of the Earth

scree broken rock fragments. Scree is usually found on mountain slopes.

soil auger thin metal tube used to obtain soil samples

soil erosion movement of soil away from where it formed. The soil is blown or washed away.

soil profile arrangement of layers in soil

terrace step cut into steep land. It can be used for growing crops.

texture what something feels like

waterlogged filled with water. A waterlogged soil has pores full of water.

weathering breaking down of rock

INDEX